Holidays

Martin Luther King, Jr. Day

by R.J. Bailey

VOLUNTEER

VOLUNTEER

Bullfrog Books

Ideas for Parents and Teachers

Bullfrog Books let children practice reading informational text at the earliest reading levels. Repetition, familiar words, and photo labels support early readers.

Before Reading

- Discuss the cover photo. What does it tell them?

- Look at the picture glossary together. Read and discuss the words.

Read the Book

- "Walk" through the book and look at the photos. Let the child ask questions. Point out the photo labels.

- Read the book to the child, or have him or her read independently.

After Reading

- Prompt the child to think more. Ask: What do you do to celebrate MLK Day? How can you help people on this day?

Bullfrog Books are published by Jump!
5357 Penn Avenue South
Minneapolis, MN 55419
www.jumplibrary.com

Library of Congress Cataloging-in-Publication Data

Names: Bailey, R.J., author.
Title: Martin Luther King Jr., Day / by R.J. Bailey.
Description: Minneapolis: Jump!, Inc. [2016]
Series: Holidays | Includes index.
Audience: Grades K–3.
Identifiers: LCCN 2016006407 (print)
LCCN 2016007032 (ebook)
ISBN 9781620313541 (hard cover: alk. paper)
ISBN 9781624964015 (e-book)
Subjects: LCSH: Martin Luther King Jr., Day—Juvenile literature. | King, Martin Luther, Jr., 1929–1968—Juvenile literature. | African Americans—Civil rights—History—20th century—Juvenile literature. | African American civil rights workers—Biography—Juvenile literature. | Civil rights workers—United States—Biography—Juvenile literature. | Baptists—United States—Clergy—Biography—Juvenile literature. | African Americans—Biography—Juvenile literature.
Classification: LCC E185.97.K5 B338 2016 (print)
LCC E185.97.K5 (ebook) | DDC 394.261—dc23
LC record available at http://lccn.loc.gov/2016006407

Editor: Kirsten Chang
Series Designer: Ellen Huber
Book Designer: Michelle Sonnek
Photo Researchers: Kirsten Chang & Michelle Sonnek

Photo Credits: Alamy, 10, 20–21, 22bl; Brandon Bourdages/Shutterstock.com, cover; Corbis, 3; Getty, 6–7, 23tl; iStock, 8–9, 12–13, 22tr, 23bl; Shutterstock, 4, 6–7, 18, 23tr, 23br; Superstock, 1, 5, 11, 14, 15, 16–17, 18–19, 22tl, 22br; Thinkstock, 24.

Printed in the United States of America at Corporate Graphics in North Mankato, Minnesota.

Table of Contents

What Is Martin Luther King, Jr. Day?

MLK Day is an American holiday.

It is in January.

It is on the third Monday.

What do we celebrate?

Dr. King led the civil rights movement.

He wanted everyone to have the same rights.

Dr. Martin Luther King, Jr.

We honor him.

How?

We help people.

Dell and Eva paint a school.

Tom builds a house.
Wow! He works hard.

We go to
a food bank.

We give food
to those in need.

We plant a tree.

14

litter

We pick up litter.

15

We go to a march.

It is in memory
of Dr. King.

Look!

Joe has a sign.

Ann reads a speech.

It is called
"I Have a Dream."

Dr. King wrote it.

It gives us hope.

I have a dream that one day this nation will rise up and live out the true meaning of its creed: "We hold these truths to be self-evident, that all men are created equal."

I have a dream that one day on the red hills of Georgia, the sons of former slaves and the sons of former slave owners will be able to sit down together at the table of brotherhood.

I have a dream that one day
Mississippi, a

OUT OF THE MOUNTAIN OF DESPAIR,
A STONE OF HOPE

We will always
remember Dr. King!

MLK Day of Service

cleaning neighborhoods

feeding the hungry

painting schools

building homes

Picture Glossary

civil rights movement
An effort by African Americans to get equal rights.

"I Have a Dream"
A speech given by Dr. Martin Luther King, Jr. on August 28, 1963.

food bank
A place where food is gathered for people who need it.

litter
Useless stuff that has been thrown away; trash.

To Learn More

Learning more is as easy as 1, 2, 3.

1) Go to www.factsurfer.com

2) Enter "MLKDay" into the search box.

3) Click the "Surf" button to see a list of websites.

With factsurfer.com, finding more information is just a click away.